Contents

Time for a treasure hunt

This teacher wants to make a display of **rough** and smooth things.

4

Is it...?
Rough or Smooth

Vic Parker

Heinemann

Little Nippers

www.heinemann.co.uk/library
Visit our website to find out more information about **Heinemann Library** books.

To order:
☎ Phone 44 (0) 1865 888066
▤ Send a fax to 44 (0) 1865 314091
▯ Visit the Heinemann Bookshop at www.heinemann.co.uk/library to browse our catalogue and order online.

First published in Great Britain by Heinemann Library, Halley Court, Jordan Hill, Oxford OX2 8EJ, part of Harcourt Education.
Heinemann is a registered trademark of Harcourt Education Ltd.

Editorial: Jilly Attwood and Claire Throp
Design: Jo Hinton-Malivoire and bigtop, Bicester, UK
Models made by: Jo Brooker
Picture Research: Rosie Garai and Sally Smith
Production: Séverine Ribierre

Originated by Dot Gradations
Printed and bound in China by South China Printing Company

ISBN 0 431 17400 8 (hardback)
08 07 06 05 04
10 9 8 7 6 5 4 3 2 1

ISBN 0 431 17405 9 (paperback)
08 07 06 05 04
10 9 8 7 6 5 4 3 2 1

British Library Cataloguing in Publication Data
Parker, Vic
Is it rough or smooth?
620.1'1292
A full catalogue record for this book is available from the British Library.

Acknowledgements
The publishers would like to thank Gareth Boden for permission to reproduce photographs.

Cover photograph reproduced with permission of Gareth Boden.

The publishers would like to thank Annie Davy for her assistance in the preparation of this book.

Every effort has been made to contact copyright holders of any material reproduced in this book. Any omissions will be rectified in subsequent printings if notice is given to the publishers.

The paper used to print this book comes from sustainable resources.

2

What can
the children
find at home?

Bristly brushes

Brush up against a brush.

The bristles are tough and **rough**.

How many different brushes can you find around the house?

Making music

Look! Some **smooth** instruments!

Search for something smooth

Ouch!

Most of these plants are prickly.

This one has smooth **soft** leaves.

What's cooking?

A grater is **rough**.

12

A rolling pin is **smooth**.

Feeling fruity

Feel some fruit with your fingers.

It's a rough, **hairy** coconut!

15

Touch paper

This paper is smooth. Slippy and slidy!

Scrapy and scratchy! This sandpaper is **rough**.

Birthday balloons

Smooth and **flat**.

Smooth and **fat**!

Taste test

Classroom display

rough things

Index

The end

Notes for adults

The *Is it . . .?* series provides young children with a first opportunity to examine and learn about common materials. The books follow a boy and girl as they go on a treasure hunt around their house to find items with contrasting textures. There are four titles in the series and when used together, the books will encourage children to express their curiosity and explore their environment. The following Early Learning Goals are relevant to this series:

Creative development
Early learning goals for exploring media and materials:
• explore colour, texture, shape, form and space in two or three dimensions
• begin to describe the texture of things.

Knowledge and understanding of the world
Early learning goals for exploration and investigation:
• investigate objects and materials by using all of their senses as appropriate
• show curiosity, observe and manipulate objects
• describe simple features of objects
• look closely at similarities, differences, patterns and change.

This book introduces the reader to a range of everyday items that are rough or smooth. It will extend young children's thinking about familiar objects and enable them to talk expressively about different materials.
The book will help children extend their vocabulary, as they will hear new words such as *display* and *bristles*. You may like to introduce and explain other new words yourself, such as *surface* and *texture*.

Follow-up activities
• Help your child improve their number ability by asking them to find ten rough things and ten smooth things around the house.
• On a trip to the supermarket, identify which fruits and vegetables are rough (e.g. cauliflower, coconut, lychee) and which are smooth (e.g. apple, mushroom, peach).
• Set up a treasure hunt for rough/smooth things around the garden by writing and hiding clues.

24